D1570663

Kate Hickey

HAVE FUN BE SAFE I LOVE YOU

...and everything else I want to say to my kids about college and beyond.

SINMIEDO
PUBLISHING

For Max and Sam

THE FRESHMAN 150

This is not a typo. The *only* number you should be focused on for the next year is The Freshman 150.

Why 150? Because that is the average number of days you'll spend at college this year. It's 150 chances to figure it out, screw it up, laugh it out, cry it out, and try it out.

150 days. Let's go.

FOREWORD

I think it's important to start off from a place of honesty: I was terrified to publish this book. Almost every day that I wrote it, I battled self doubt, self-worth, and fear. The most prevalent questions on replay in my head at all hours of the day:

Who will read it?
Who do I think I am to write a book?
Is this information even new or important?
What will people think?

 The answers turned out to be:
Who cares?
Someone who loves to write and help people.
We'll find out.
I can't care.

Growing up, my youngest brother Luke used to say "I can't care," pronounced very nasally and as one word. */kan·keer/*

Besides it being adorable, I also find the phrase to be so poignant. Way too deep for a four-year-old, but I love that it implies a sense of action.

Instead of "I don't care," which suggests that we're without empathy — it's more about choosing not to care. Better yet, an outright *refusal* to care. I can't care.

I can't care what people think of me or it will rob me of myself and my purpose. I can't care if this book sells two copies and both are bought by my dad. I can't care because if I do — what's left for me?

Also, if I don't write a book, how will Kristen Wiig and Oprah ever find me and befriend me and call me up to talk about my ideas for radically changing the US educational system?

They won't.

The answer is that it's not about why I should write this book, it's more about what if I don't write this book? I will have failed myself, I will regret it, and I will always wonder "what if?" Also, I will be asking those around me to live without fear, but not holding myself to that same standard. That's crap.

Young me cared way too much about conventional success, recognition, and image. Wiser me knows that the time and energy I spent worrying and comparing was a complete waste.

This new "can't care" me is a fearless female author and I like doing life with her. I wish we'd met decades ago.

In the end, I've sat with my doubts and moved past them. It has been a daily struggle that will likely continue way past my publication date.

A whole new fear of "have people accepted my work?" will be my next chapter.

I picture myself reading bad Amazon reviews and cursing strangers: "This a-hole is criticizing my book, but can't even spell *their*?!!" I'll get real petty and hurt and then I'll move through that rejection and fear too. I can't care.

I'm telling you all this to say: I'm here with you. I'm not going to give you any "go be the difference in the world" or "dance like nobody's watching" BS when I'm not willing to do the hard stuff myself.

So here we go, friends. A book on how to live your best

college life while coexisting and moving through self-doubt. Practicing while preaching.

We can't care.

ABOUT THE BOOK

This next chapter in your life will fall somewhere between the panic of "I have four years to figure out my entire future" and the party-mode internal switch that flips when you hear the beat drop in your favorite song.

Quite the spread.

Lots of pressure is put on you in your early 20s as you step out on your own.

You'll be trying to figure out what you want to do with the rest of your life, sculpting who you are and who you want to be, and navigating how to live on your own. Those are three pretty big asks of someone at any age.

This book is designed to unpack and demystify each of those three categories and is set up in those same sections:

Sculpting who you are and who you want to be:
Part 1 — On Building Yourself

Navigating how to live on your own and practical advice for classes, professors, books and more:
Part 2 — On Slaying Your College Days

Figure out what you want to do with the rest of your life:
Part 3 — On Building Your Career

This book is titled *Have Fun, Be Safe, I Love You* because after fun, safety, and love — the rest are just details.

All of the advice in this book is general. It does not take into account your story, your truth, or your history. It is meant to be a broad guide and a collection of advice from recent college graduates, anecdotes to make you laugh, and quotes to get you through. So, scribble in the margins, underline, doodle, send pics to your friend, and tear pages out.

There is no one-size-fits-all approach to life. Take what you need and leave what you don't.

CONTENTS

PART ONE

ON BUILDING YOURSELF

ONE BLACK COW

Upon her arrival at Texas Tech, my mom wanted to be a veterinarian. On day one, jacked up on that freshman energy, the incoming vet-hopefuls were led by the professor into an agriculture center. In the middle of a dusty rodeo ring stood one black cow.

The students gathered around the cow, obliviously standing with its head hung amongst the giddy freshman, awaiting the professor's instructions for cow anatomy and vocabulary. Instead, the professor pulled out a gun from his white lab coat and shot the cow, point-blank, between the eyes.

Convulsing, the cow dropped slowly to its knees with a thud.

My mom started crying hysterically and ran back to her dorm room to call her dad.

"Dad!! No. I can't do this — I just saw a cow get shot in the face! I don't want to be a vet. I mean, I think I do. Actually, I hate cats. Uhhhh, I just want to be a vet to help big dogs...not the small, yappy ones either. I don't know what to do, Dad."

Calmly, my grandfather instructed her to do one thing:

"Find the school's listing of courses and circle all of the classes that interest you. Sign up today for all the classes that you think look fun," he said.

My mom did as instructed, and enrolled in a photography class among a few other new courses.

Photography quickly became her thing and everyone from

her college days remembers my mom with a camera around her neck. After graduating, she went on to work in a photo studio, became a photojournalist, and eventually the Managing Editor of our local newspaper.

Don't wait for a cow murder moment to shock you into a new direction. Whether or not you are dead set on a path, be open to new things. Changing your major or changing your mind does not mean you're floundering, wasting money or time — it's an important part of the process of finding what you love to do.

Your support group might not be as understanding or as wise as my mom's dad, but this story is your green light to try all the things.

Photography has shaped my mom as a person and it's all because she was given explicit permission to "try something that sounds fun." Give yourself that license.

IN ME I TRUST

"I want to tell my college freshman self that the expectation of 'The college experience' is bullshit. Your college experience is the college experience. Everyone is different and that's what it's all about. Get out of your head with expectations and just focus on you."
Tierney Pine
University of Tennessee

College is not about finding the perfect job or the perfect partner. It's not even about finding yourself. That's way too lofty a goal. College is for breaking away from the life that has been designed and structured for you and creating and experimenting with what makes you happy and whole. What fills your bucket? What do you stand for? What energies do you allow into your sacred space?

As you navigate your course, make sure that no one else's map is in your hands.

This is awkward, I have sold you a book about "what to do in college" but the best advice is to not follow any path but your own. In fact, I'm telling you to drop out of college if you feel that is your true north.

While this may sound daunting or abstract, the best way to start this new chapter is not to compare yourself, your journey, experience, or story with anyone.

If you can work on doing this, and yes it will be daily work, college will become uniquely and beautifully yours. Trust yourself that you know what you need. Stop asking people what they think. Stop comparing.

Wholly trust yourself with your life decisions.

THE 10%

My first job as a teacher was in a high school for unconventional learners, which turned out to mean students who were scarred, creative, reluctant, unique, and extremely brave.

On the whole, these kids hated school because it wasn't designed for them and they were right. For some, they were ignored year after year by teachers and administrators and lacked confidence in their abilities. Generally, they were wildly creative and talented, but most schools don't know what to do with students who don't fit into a box.

I was 26 and my students were 19 so I knew my first impression was a make-or-break moment. I very carefully selected my first-day-of-school outfit: a black skirt that read chic but not boring, a fuschia blouse which meant I was fun, and bold earrings showing that I had edge so they could relate to me. I was Robin Williams and they were about to be my *Dead Poets Society*.

I was an immediate disaster. After going to the bathroom and walking the halls, I sat down on my black office chair and for some reason I could actually feel the whole of my butt cheek on the cool pleather. I had tucked my skirt into the top of my thong waistband and walked the entirety of the hall baring my right ass cheek.

Also, my last name is Hickey, so there's that.

For months, the students tested me, heckled me, and

avoided work at all costs. I had one kid scrawl "F*ck You" on every single fill-in-the-blank of his Spanish test. He spelled it right and I always said "never leave any blanks" so I think I gave him a 12% to throw him off. They were really going the extra mile to hate me.

I cried almost every day. I took up a casual smoking habit while blaring angry rap on my commute home, fantasizing about clever phrases I could say to them without losing my job.

My husband saw that I was a wreck, and knew to stay out of my way because, dammit, I was going to save these kids.

In the throes of that taxing year, I received the best life advice from my mentor, Ron. The phrase has stuck with me for decades. It got me through subsequent jobs, relationships, an election, and has, sort of, become my mantra when times are tough:

Only 10% of people are jackasses. Don't let the jackasses take over.

Something clicked. It really wasn't all of my students that needed dog cursing, it was only three to four kids in each period. The majority were lost or silenced by the jackasses. The jackasses had taken over, and I needed to stop focusing on their antics and start teaching to the other 90% of students who only mildly disliked me.

This advice has shifted my perspective and shaped my view on the world. The buttholes are the minority, yet we somehow allow them to take up the majority of our head and heart space.

Why do we always focus on the negative? Because it's more glaring, disappointing, infuriating, and frustrating. It zaps our good energy and consumes our thoughts. It's called negativity bias and it's a real thing. It's why we remember insults more than praise and why one crap moment, in a 12-hour day, makes us label the whole day as "a bad day".

Our negativity bias is part of our evolutionary survival as a species and it's what keeps us alive and attune to danger. Today, that negativity bias isn't keeping us from being attacked by wolves — it's just stealing our joy and eroding our happiness, one negative thought at a time.

How do we reclaim our thoughts and feelings? Ignore negative self-talk, give extra and intentional gratitude for the good moments, and don't allow your mind to replay or fixate on the bad stuff.

Ninety percent of people are doing things right, following rules, and doing their best. Most of your day is perfectly fine. Don't let the jackasses take over your life — or your mind.

Follow up: I didn't end up saving those kids, per se. I did give them the tools, attention, and love so that they could save themselves. I still am proud of who they continue to become and I still curse our antiquated educational system that is designed for one kind of learner. That's another book entirely.

Also, "F-you-boy" ended up apologizing to me and thanking me for my patience.

Sometimes ignoring the jackass is what un-jacks their ass.

"Only 10% of people are jackasses. Don't let the jackasses take over."

Ron Heady

DITCH THE DRAINERS

For the next decade, you will be surrounded by people who are all discovering themselves, growing, and changing. Naturally, this will happen at differing paces for everyone.

Stay on your toes with your friendships because some friends will be discovering yoga and veganism while others will be discovering whippets and coke. Another group of people will be doing nothing at all and their lack of discovery needs to be your discovery.

You will likely have to end friendships with people you now consider your closest confidants. While this seems harsh and sad, it's just the ebb and flow of life. Distance, drugs, politics, work ethics, relationships, money, and time are all factors that will likely play into why some friendships will fizzle out. While it will hurt to let go of some of your most treasured people, try not to take it personally.

There's a fine line between loyalty and self-preservation, and if you're on the fence about someone — just ask yourself how you feel after spending a few hours with that person. Do you feel lighter and inspired or annoyed and exhausted? If it's the latter, they've got to go.

Surrounding yourself with people that grow, challenge and encourage you is crucial to your success. While moving on from some people can feel like you're being disloyal, hear this: you can be disloyal to them or to yourself. Never choose the latter.

It's hard to part, but you've got to ditch the people that drain you. Mute, unfollow, and block anyone that steals your joy. Be a ruthless editor of friends.

"You can't keep getting mad at
people sucking the life out of you
if you keep giving them the straw."

Unknown

BE A KAREN

During my sophomore year, I was SO excited to get out of the dorms and into an apartment. My downstairs dorm mate, Karen, was also leaving Holden Hall and was headed for the freedom land of co-ed apartments, where kegs were encouraged and curfews were not.

I already had the perfect poster placement in my head and a set of dishes picked out at Target.

"Should we go visit a few apartments this weekend?" I asked her.

She clearly was not on my matching bedspread level because all Karen said was: "I can't be your roommate."

This bishhhhh. I was so hurt and confused. How could I have so grossly misjudged our friendship?

"I want to be your friend, so I can't be your roommate," she explained.

Oh ok...well that's worse, thank you. I was so hurt.

Turns out I got an apartment with another hallmate who quickly became my best friend, and later my maid of honor, and the Godmother to my daughter. Suck on that Karen.

Actually, Karen and I remain great friends too. She knew that if we were going to be friends that we couldn't room together. Karen had the foresight to know that our habits and/or personalities would clash and we might jeopardize a good thing.

It's sort of like how you should never work at a restaurant you love because it will ruin it for you. (Everyone who has worked in foodservice is nodding their head.)

Be a Karen. Think through your friends' ice chewing habits, finances, ambitions, grades, and partners before allowing them into your quality world.

Instead of slowly resenting your people for eating your last taquito or staining your jeans, set clear boundaries.

It's not personal — it's honesty, transparency, and true friendship.

> ## "Boundaries are the distance at which I can love you and me simultaneously."
> *Prentis Hemphill*

QUESTION WHAT YOU THINK YOU KNOW

*"Talk to as many people who are different from
you as you possibly can."*
Gary Baker
Rowan University

One of the most beautiful parts of this chapter in your life will
be your realization of the myriad of ways in which life can be
lived. Challenge yourself to step out of how you were raised
and the relationships that formed you. Listen to dissenting
viewpoints, experience differences in religion, race, and social
norms with an open mind.

The best part about your college experience will not take
place in the classroom. It will be in late night conversations and
through meaningful and diverse relationships.

If you get an invite to someone's home to meet their family —
always take it.

Pretty sure most of our world's problems with hatred and
misunderstanding could be solved if we all just ate a meal at
each other's homes.

Question what you think you know. It doesn't mean you can't
return to your roots — it means you can determine for yourself
who you want to be.

"Keep an open mind; it's the only way new things can get in."

Colleen Hoover

COMMUNICATION 101

If you are having a problem with someone, be honest and direct. It's that simple.

No need to spend time worrying what you think they're thinking. No projecting. Ask the tough questions and have a chat.

The drama sets in when assumptions mix with self-doubt. Your head chatter turns negative and extreme as time goes on and a false narrative builds in your head.

Texting has no tone, so having hard conversations face-to-face is crucial.

Ask, listen, and don't avoid difficult talks. You'll save a lot of time, relationships, and energy.

"Bad communication ends
a lot of good things."

SCARFACE

In an experiment conducted at Dartmouth College, psychologist Dr. Robert Cleck proves an interesting point about our inability to accurately perceive ourselves (Blakeslee).

In the experiment, subjects were to attend a party after they were given gnarly fake scars on their foreheads with makeup.

The experiment was to see how the scar would affect the way that people treated them. The subjects were told to observe how people spoke to them and to see if there was any noticeable difference while wearing the scar.

Plot twist: Right before the party began, pretending to need one final touch-up, the makeup artists actually *removed the scar entirely* just before the subjects entered the party. They thought they looked gross but they were completely normal.

The "scar faces" were interviewed after they mixed and mingled at the party. The results: The subjects all felt that partygoers were indeed staring at their scars and some even claimed that people were averting their gaze, so as not to stare at the gash on their face (that wasn't there).

The point: We all think we are so good at reading others' non-verbal cues, when in fact, our insecurities and self-consciousness are often in control.

How many times have you thought someone was mad at you, only to find out they had their phone notifications off, they were sick, or out of town?

The quicker you can realize "most people are not thinking about you," the happier and lighter you will feel.

You do not have a scar on your face. Even if you did, most people are too worried about their own fake scars to notice yours.

"You wouldn't worry so much about what others think of you if you realized how seldom they do."

Eleanor Roosevelt

IF YOU WANT TO BE COOL, DO COOL STUFF

"If you want to be the main character, you also have to be the author."
Evan Esworthy
Northumbria University

Our habits define us. If you want to know more about the world, you'll have to read the news. If you want to be interesting, you'll have to do interesting things. While that may feel daunting, it's not as hard as you'd think.

Create small daily habits and soon you will be a person that does that thing.

Read for pleasure 20 minutes a day and you'll be well-read. Run three times a week and before you know it, you're a runner. Practice guitar every Sunday and in a couple of years, you'll be able to shred.

If you want to speak French, minor in it, and don't be afraid to start from square one. If you want to be well-traveled, start with one trip.

Daily decisions compound over time. The secret to success is your daily habits.

ABSOLUTELY NO BOYS

During the summer before my junior year of college, I studied abroad in Spain. Like a bad rom com, I discovered that it was finally time to ditch my high school boyfriend and discover the world. I came back from that summer tan, liberated, and as obnoxious as a 20-year-old back from study abroad.

I made a promise to myself that I would not get into a relationship. I just wanted to be free and focus on my goals. Ambition would be my date until graduation. Absolutely no boys.

Two weeks after my return from Spain, I went to a party thrown by some mutual friends. It was a "wine and cheese" party and the boys required formal attire. The wine was in boxes, neckties were clipped on, and the music was at a volume where we could actually converse. Well played, boys.

An hour in, I was chatting in a small group, and one short guy in an ill-fitting olive green suit caught my attention. He was explaining his internship with the NBA, and I was impressed. After a while, the crowd peeled off and it was just him and me left talking. Sober and beaming, he looked me right in the eyes and cut me off mid-sentence.

"I want to date the shit out of you," he said.

Well, hot dog. He was ambition in human form. I was making no compromises with this guy. He was smiley, direct, driven, funny, kind, pint-size, and perfect for me.

I told him that night that if he stood in the way of me

completing my bucket list, we were not going to work. We vowed to help each other accomplish our dreams as a team, and I married the shit out of him three years later.

To this day, we continue to check one thing off of our bucket lists each year. Marathons, helicopter rides, children, bungee jumping, moving to Europe, and writing a book are just a few of our Team Hickey accomplishments.

You've got 80 years to find "the one" — not four.

This is a time in your life where you can be happily unattached. Enjoy that freedom and try not to wish it away. Focus on your bucket list and on becoming the best version of yourself. The real magic happens when we stop searching outside ourselves.

So, if you just happen to meet someone that deserves a seat on your fun bus — let them on very cautiously. The moment they slow the ride down or try to grab your steering wheel — kick them off. You are crafting your best self and loading your fun bus full of memories, experiences, and people that give you joy. You are the driver. Beep beep, bitches.

MENTAL HYGIENE

*"Take care of your mental health. To accomplish the goals you have
in life, it is almost impossible if you have underlying issues that you
internalize or ignore. Those emotions will never go away and
you'll be dragged down by them forever."*
Faith Hendrickson

Part of forging your own path and becoming independent means
that you need to prioritize and practice good mental hygiene.

I'm using the phrase mental hygiene and not mental health
because hygiene implies a need for regular upkeep. Similar
to washing your face and putting on deodorant, your feelings,
energies, and thoughts deserve the same amount of daily attention.

Ways to maintain good mental hygiene:

* Journal
* Use a daily de-stressor app
* Unfollow people on social media that trigger any negative
  emotions for you
* Limit alcohol (it is a massive depressant and causes anxiety)
* See a counselor online or in-person regularly
* Be vulnerable with your trusted friends
* Avoid starting your day with social media
* Reward yourself when you've reached a goal or stopped a

bad mental habit (like negative self-talk)
- Find an on-campus or virtual support group
- Practice positive self-talk
- Schedule downtime
- Take a walk, swim, practice yoga, move your body
- Leave space in your schedule to create or to do what brings you joy
- Say no to things and people that don't serve you

Mental hygiene is just for upkeep, like brushing your teeth. Some of us have stuck emotions or real trauma that require full-on root canals.

If this is you, spend time and energy healing. Moving into this next chapter of your life will be nearly impossible if you have a disorder or chemistry imbalance that is undiagnosed.

Seek help with an advisor, therapist, or counselor as there are lots of on-campus resources for treatment. Stay encouraged and get help. You've got this.

Mental hygiene needs to be a priority for you to succeed as a person and to find joy in your life. It will help attract healthy relationships and help you stay balanced under the stress of school and change.

Self-care isn't spa days and champagne — it's a daily decision to get good sleep, move your body, and talk to yourself with love and grace.

"Don't believe everything you think."

NOSEDIVES ARE NORMAL

Chances are high that you'll spiral: Skip one assignment and it will give you anxiety so you'll lose sleep and miss class, then another assignment and another class, and suddenly you're so anxious about this loss of control that you can't even muster the energy to get out of bed or hit "next song" on your playlist.

Socializing will seem impossible. Decision-making is out of the question because choosing between chicken or beef ramen will require a Herculean effort.

Over-sleeping and negative self-talk will start to feel normal and you'll make excuses to others as to why you don't want to do anything.

You know you're seriously off, but you can't fix it.

Likely no one notices. It's not even that hard to hide. No, you can't just go for a walk and feel better. You need help.

My junior year of college, I lost my shit. I was so sad, lost, and nothing felt good.

I tried friends, parties, decorating my room, eating right, eating wrong, and lots of extra sleep but nothing worked.

After months, which felt like years, I called my Mom. I needed her to come to school and get me. Where were we going? No idea. I needed to figure this out. She drove to get me, God love her, and sat on my bed watching me bawl — the crying that involves your shoulders and face muscles that you didn't know you had.

She helped me sift through what the problems were, and it didn't seem like there were any so we started looking for causes instead. Turns out it was my birth control pills. I stopped taking them that day and felt like myself again in less than a week.

I hope your fix is this simple. Whatever you do, ask for help. Seek someone out. Resources are available on campus if you feel like your shoulder-heaving sobs don't belong with friends or family.

Your lack of drive or decision-making is not who you are — it's likely just the season you're in.

"Don't confuse a bad day with a bad life."

PRETENDING TO DO LIFE

"Three quarters of all mental health conditions occur before age 25."
Ken Duckworth
*Chief Medical Officer, National Alliance
of Mental Health ("Asking for Help")*

Depression and anxiety are very easy to hide. My out-of-control birth control moment was months of silent suffering and internal panic. I cast myself as the leading role in a play called "Pretending To Do Life." This act fooled even my closest friends, but I crumpled backstage after every exhaustive daily performance.

According to a study by the Journal of Adolescent Health, "Suicidal thinking, severe depression and rates of self-injury among U.S. college students more than doubled over less than a decade." (Joseph).

This is scary. We need each other.

Asking: "Are you ok?" is not enough.

All of my fellow "Pretending to Do Life" co-stars know how to answer that question: "I'm ok," we lie. We take our bow and bury ourselves in our covers and self-loathing.

Be persistent with friends that aren't showing up. Tell someone. Make them get out of bed and talk to you. Give them some on-campus mental health resources. Seek learning accommodations from the school. Remind them that you are there and that you love them.

In college, and in life, you can be surrounded by people but still feel extremely lonely.

DON'T COMMIT TOO QUICK

When my son, Max, started fifth grade at a new public school in Spain, he didn't speak *any* Spanish. I was short on wise words for him as I knew the first few months would be really hard. I played it cool, but inside I was panicking for him. As you know, middle-schoolers can be real assholes.

My only advice was that he not throw himself at any one group too quickly. I asked that he sit back and observe everyone's behavior and personality, and then make a decision on who he would let into his quality world. Easy enough, as all he could do was basically play charades and point at things like a caveman.

In Spain, kids get copious amounts of playtime during the school day, like over two hours. This is great when you have friends, but an eternity when you're alone. So Max ignored my advice and headed straight for the kid with the newest Nikes and freshest fade. We'll call him Roberto.

"Hola enemigo," cool Roberto said to Max with an outstretched hand.

"Hola," Max replied excitedly, thinking he heard "amigo" meaning friend.

In fact, "enemigo" means enemy and Max shook this little prick's hand setting into motion a sizable fifth grade rivalry that lasted two trimesters.

Try not to commit yourself to any one relationship or group

too quickly.

Greek life is a great way to build a network and have a built-in social calendar. However, fraternities and sororities can sometimes be an extension of high school, which means a new, large faction of people with expectations of your time, behavior, and money. While there are great opportunities for leadership and philanthropy in sororities and fraternities, just make sure you're joining for the right reasons.

Having a few fun friends in your hallway is a great start but don't put all your eggs in their basket either.

Shop around.

Before you pledge yourself fully to one group, ask yourself why. If the answer is "community" or "belonging" or a "fun social life" — give yourself some time, and try creating that on your own terms first. You will surprise yourself.

Soon enough, you will have multiple factions of friends and social prospects that will rival any organized fraternal or on-campus event.

Don't shake too early with an "enemigo" or you'll spend semesters shaking off a bad start.

"You are not for everyone."

MOST DAYS ARE TUESDAYS

Now that you are out of the high school halls, few people will care about what you're doing, wearing, or saying, besides your parents and a handful of loyal friends. It's not you, it's just life.

High school usually provides lots of fun distractions that you didn't even realize made the ordinary days feel "special." Gone are spirit weeks, pep rallies, and your familiar seat in the lunchroom.

For some, this might come as a huge relief as that was never their bag. However, the rhythm of high school is marked with mini-milestones, events, and activities. Whether you enjoyed them or not, this demarcation made the days pass with some familiarity.

Stay encouraged. You'll soon find new normals that will make your next chapter fun too.

In the meantime, find beauty in the mundane and meaning in the little stuff. It will make for happy days and a fulfilled life.

Fridays are exciting for a reason — because every other day is just a Tuesday.

"Think back to times when you were super anxious. Did it ever turn out as bad as you thought? No, because most of what we are afraid of happening never actually happens. And on the rare chance it does, it's never as bad as you thought."

My Yoga teacher
but I forgot her name

LET GO

"I've stopped trying to control different situations and pushed myself to go with the flow. I'm saying 'yes' more and doing uncomfortable things. When I let things go, it works out best."
Abbi Greenwood
Gap Year Adventurer in Spain

Skinny-dip. Preferably in a lake or ocean and bonus points for a long sunny afternoon on a topless beach. Celebrate your healthy body, own it, show it off to yourself. (Wear sunscreen though, even on the nips. If your golden globes have never seen the sun they will burn up like fried chicken.)

If skinny-dipping isn't your version of free and brave, find what is. Hop in the car at midnight for a spontaneous road trip or surprise someone with a day of cellphone-less adventure.

Create wild and beautiful stories to tell your grandkids or secrets you keep to remind yourself you're fearless.

"One day your life will flash before your eyes. Make sure it's worth watching."

Gerard Way

YOUR GUT IS YOUR GUIDE

In the book *The Gift of Fear*, author Gavin de Becker talks about the complexity of fear. He explains that humans are the only species on earth to rationalize their fear and ignore their gut instincts.

He gives a great example: A woman enters an elevator alone at night and "ding" the doors open. A man enters alone and smells of alcohol. He's making her nervous and staring at her with a stern and almost scary look.

Instead of tuning into her instincts and exiting the elevator, she stays and rationalizes her fear. "I don't want to hurt his feelings and get off right when he gets on. That's so rude." Or, "I don't want him to think that I'm judging his appearance. He might have an addiction or ailment. That's mean of me."

The book goes on to demonstrate that time and time again before people are assaulted or attacked, they experience a moment of fear and knowing that something bad was going to happen. As humans, we are the only species that allow our thoughts to override our gut instincts.

Animals hear a twig break, they run. They see a large shadowy figure at the watering hole, they gone.

Would you rather risk hurting a stranger's feelings, or save yourself? Do you want to "not be rude" at a party or end up in real trouble? There's never a downside to following your gut.

Listen to your intuition and when your body gifts you fear,

silence the "nice" voices in your head that are rationalizing your actions. If it feels sketchy, you're right.

TURKEY DROP

"College is the first time you get to really make your own decisions and the last time you don't have major responsibilities so don't let a relationship dictate your choices."
Carlye Grandy
Auburn University

The phrase "Turkey Drop" is used for high school couples that only last until the first Thanksgiving of freshman year. This breakup has a nickname for a reason. Making a high school relationship work in college requires lots of trust, communication, and work.

I'm not saying you can't try, you just can't compromise your experience or growth for anyone else. Your energy, focus, time, and experience are non-negotiable. The most important relationship right now is the one you have with yourself. Period.

Whatever you decide, try not to spend too much time salvaging a relationship unless it's really, really worth it. Jealousy, long phone calls, missing time with friends, nights where you're nervous to do you because it will result in too much explaining later... these are signs that you're whispering on the phone in a quiet corner of the room when you should be on the dance floor.

Your person can be wonderful and hold you back. That's what makes the right decision extra hard. Instead of thinking of it as a breakup, position it to yourself as a commitment to your college experience.

If someone is keeping you from meeting new people, saying yes, and experiencing college — they've got to go. Drop that turkey and don't even wait until November. Halloween drop.

"It's difficult to undergo a personal transformation while you're surrounded by people who knew who you used to be."
Mitchell Earl

KNOW YOUR LIMITS

Have fun. This is your time to enjoy your freedom and friends.

Just remember to look out for yourself. Part of exploring joy is knowing your limits. Only you will know what is excessive and unhealthy and that doesn't always look the same for everyone. Drinking, drugs, sex, food, spending, video games, and your cell phone will tempt you daily. Learn where your boundaries are and check yourself. If any of these vices become escapes from reality or affect you physically or mentally, you could be causing yourself serious and permanent damage.

My sophomore year I received two Minor in Possession charges for underage drinking. (Yes mom, two. Don't be mad) I thought it was no big deal at the time until I had to appear in court, find a lawyer, and years later apply to get my teaching license. Because I would be working with minors, I had to appeal to the State of Michigan with a detailed statement and jump through legal hoops to get my charges expunged (great word). Those lukewarm Natty Lights could have cost me my career. So dumb.

I won't preach about drunk driving or alcohol-related dangers but I will give you a few statistics. These statistics represent someone's daughter, best friend, or boyfriend and they were likely all students who thought they could totally handle themselves.

According to CollegeDrinkingPrevention.com

("Consequences", 2022):

- Each year 1,519 college students between the ages of 18 and 24 die from alcohol-related unintentional injuries, including motor-vehicle crashes.
- Every year 696,000 students between the ages of 18 and 24 are assaulted by another student who has been drinking
- Researchers have confirmed a long-standing finding that 1 in 5 college women experience sexual assault during their time in college. A majority of sexual assaults in college involve alcohol or other substances.

Accidents happen by accident. You are not invincible. Have fun and be safe.

WHY YOU CAN'T KICK AMBER OUT OF THE PARTY

"When I was in high school I felt like I shape-shifted too much.
In order to be real, speak your opinions, stand up,
and don't feel the need to be agreeable all the time.
This is your chance to create your authentic self."
Julia Cohen
Florida State University

Of all my college shenanigans, for some strange reason, I am particularly ashamed of one night. It wasn't throwing up a rainbow of jello shots on our bathroom wall — I could at least blame vodka for that. Instead, it was a stone-cold sober decision to be a big 'ole bitch. It's a mistake that followed me after college because it had to come after me to teach me a lesson. More on that later.

My friends were mad at a girl named Amber from some old high school drama, so I thought I would prove my loyalty to them. We were not going to let Amber into the Beta house party.

At least 50 people were lined up on the lawn to get in. I can't remember the excuse I used to keep her out but I'm sure it was vile and untrue. She left embarrassed and stunned but I was "in" with my new hallmates.

Gross. That's what wanting to fit in does and it does not stop in high school. In fact, it happens in teacher's lounges, hair salons, and professional corporations all over the world every day. Fully functioning adults are just grown high school kids who never learned this lesson.

I've bent my authenticity, quieted my true feelings, or hopped on the bandwagon way too many times. The desire to fit in is *human* and has no age. Why is that?! Because being authentic is hard and soul-searching work.

It took me compromising myself again in my 30s to finally learn my lesson and it's something I wish I learned earlier.

These answers will not come in a big revelation or moment in time. They will slowly show up in a dozen little moments and conversations where you will catch yourself: "Wait. Is *this* what I want? Is this *me*?"

Inauthenticity can slowly erode your character and self-esteem and there's a high price to pay — even if the check doesn't come until years later.

Authenticity requires lots of practice and lots of pauses and a big long painful look in the mirror.

Are you shrinking to make people feel better? Are you being loyal to a group of people that just sit around and shit-talk? Are you kicking Amber out of the party when all you really want is to go back to your dorm room and watch a movie and order Jimmy Johns?

PROFESSOR MCMURDER

Back to the rodeo ring and the Texas cow murder incident.

While slightly insane, that veterinary professor knew what he was doing. He had probably seen herds of students like my mom: Animal people who love their labrador, but who never thought of the day-to-day realities of the job. He was showing those freshmen that death is a big part of caring for animals.

He saved them semesters of money and energy by hitting the fast-forward button to the daily grind of life as a vet: sterilization surgeries, stomach extractions of weird shit your dog ate, and my personal fave — anal gland lancing!

Before you commit to a major, think about how you want to spend your days. What is it that you are doing when you lose track of time? What brings you joy? What are you good at? What would you do for free?

If you want to live abroad, go into a field that will allow for a digital nomad lifestyle like marketing, photography, graphic design, or web development.

If being in nature is where you're happy — think surveying land, National Park Service jobs, water conservation, landscape architecture, or any job that will get you outdoors.

The trick is not to think about what will bring you money, status, or stability in the future, but to think about what you love to do *right now*. The future will work itself out when you follow your passion.

If you are still struggling to figure out your passion, so are people of every age. Just start somewhere. Even if you spend a year trying something only to discover it's not for you, that realization counts as fantastic progress too.

BE SAD WITH ME

Every day, I pick up my nine-year-old daughter, Sam, from school and we walk home together. It's a rare time in our day where we are one-on-one without distractions for 20 minutes of walking and talking.

Upon approaching the school, I do the same two things to ready myself for her exit:

1. Get off the phone

2. Remind myself to shut up

For almost one mile of walking and rolling her pink school backpack through people and traffic, she absolutely dumps on me. Playground "drama," the lunch monitor's misunderstanding of ketchup ratios to chicken nuggets, the song she made up with her friends, all the things.

Probably one-third of our walks are the result of her having held everything in at school and then exploding.

I listen and when she's finished, I ask: "Do you want me to say anything or just feel sad with you?"

"Feel sad with me, Mama."

Then we go home, eat a couple Oreos and watch people unwrap slime on YouTube, as one does.

As an over-sharer, helper, fixer, lover, and know-it-all in

recovery, it takes everything inside me not to give her advice. I want to tell her stories of the time that "this exact same thing happened to me" and how I dealt with it. I want to protect her nuggets by offering to send wee little ketchup packets in her school bag. I fight my desire to control, advise, and insert my life into hers. It takes everything in me to shut up and say, "what do you want me to do?"

Nine times out of ten, she says "just feel sad with me."

True listening is a lost art. We're on the phone, in the car, on a run, in line, baby talking our animals, shushing people, and forever waiting for our turn to interject. Let's just shut up and sit silently in sadness together sometimes.

1. Get off the phone.

2. Shut up.

3. Ask "Do you want me to say anything or just feel sad with you?"

YOUR WAY IS THE WAY

"Use this transition to reinvent yourself in every way you were scared to in high school. Do you and leave the expectations of who you should hang out with and what you should do back at home."
Tanner Koza
Auburn University

You are under no obligation to make sense to anyone, this includes your parents. The reality is most parents just want their kids to end up being happy, and the details of how they get there are not important.

Other people might be in your head about what the college experience should be, what it was for them, and what they want it to be for you. You are not living their life.

"Every time you're given a choice between disappointing someone else and disappointing yourself, your duty is to disappoint that someone else. Your job, throughout your entire life, is to disappoint as many people as it takes to avoid disappointing yourself."

Glennon Doyle

FLOWER POWER

If you were to invest in only ONE pair of shoes for the rest
of your life — you would do some serious research and be
very selective. You would likely consider a sensible style that
could carry you through all seasons and outfits. Quality of
construction and cost wouldn't be a dealbreaker. You'd try the
shoes on, walk around in them, read reviews, and really think
about your purchase. These would be your only shoes for the
rest of your life! Is this white chunky sneaker me *right now* or
me *forever*?

Treat a tattoo exactly like this. Getting inked in a time when
you are still building your identity might be a permanent choice
for the temporary you.

Let's reflect: What is the first thing you ask when you see
someone with a tattoo? It's usually: "What does that mean or
represent?"

Make sure you are cool to answer this question about your
tat approximately four million times and that you'll be proud of
that answer in the year 2075.

The other question you might ask a tatted person: "When
did you get that?" This translates to "When did you make THAT
mistake?!" The inquirer knows that you don't love the Looney
Toons Tweety Bird, so this is the low-key way to ask for your
story of regret. These stories are usually pretty funny, which is
why we are ballsy enough to ask in the first place.

Here's mine:

When my parents moved our family from Texas to Michigan, I was in the middle of my sophomore year of high school. I wanted a tattoo so badly, and my mom finally caved because she felt so guilty about the move.

New in town, we drove to a sketchy head shop in Ypsilanti, Michigan. I had not planned on mom saying yes and had absolutely no strong convictions at the ripe old age of 16. I didn't have a clue as to what I wanted and was thumbing through the design binders nervously.

The gnarly shop employees were blaring death metal and I could barely see through the pages for the thick cloud of cigarette smoke. My mom blurted out after all of three minutes: "Just PICK something, Kate! This place is disgusting!"

Errr, ok. I didn't want her to change her mind so I quickly pointed to a morning glory flower and chose the color yellow for the yellow rose of Texas. (what?!) It's on my hip and has stayed hidden under clothes from age 19 to today. That flower bloomed like a mother effer when I had kids and I'm so grateful it's in a place where I never have to look at it unless I'm in the shower.

Looking back, what I really wanted was new friends and I thought that the tattoo would make me look hard. This was 1997 and tattoos were not nearly as common, so it did win me some street cred in the hard school hallways of Saline, Michigan ... for about 20 minutes.

Whatever you decide, don't get a bargain. Pay money for a quality piece from an experienced artist. Make sure this tattoo is the now you and the future you.

OLIVIA'S BALLOON

A bucket list is setting words to your adventures. It's penning your desires and dreams and finding the exact words for what's inside of you.

You have to write or type out your bucket list — it's the first step to manifesting your dreams. Don't just write a list of countries to visit either, put down things you want to learn, taste, see, change, and accomplish.

As a teacher, each year I had my students write down their bucket lists and, most importantly, share them with each other.

I posted the lists for months in my classroom as a sort of "compass north" so that they would be reminded of their goals and would remain inspired to go after them.

A few months after this lesson, one of my sweetest students received the news that her grandfather had passed. She was also dealing with an alcoholic and abusive family member on top of the hormonal hell that is high school.

As a class, we felt compelled to show Olivia that she was seen and loved. Someone pulled her bucket list off the wall. Reading through it we noticed that she wanted to ride a hot air balloon. "We can do this," I said.

For over a week, we collected money for her and I found a coupon for a local balloon company. We decided that a hot air balloon ride alone is no fun, so we raised enough money for a ticket for two.

When Olivia returned to school we had written her whole bucket list on the whiteboard in what must have been 800pt font. We blindfolded her and handed her a dry erase marker.

Full of pride and excitement, we guided her to the words "Ride a hot air balloon" on the whiteboard. Hand-in-hand, we crossed off those words and removed her blindfold.

Crying and overwhelmed by the gesture, and for the first time in school, Olivia felt surrounded by people that cared.

Make a bucket list. Have faith in people. Believe that others want to see you succeed. Put your goals out there. Even if you're too scared or poor to cross things off of your list, help your favorite people into their hot air balloons.

Manifest that shit.

PART TWO

ON SLAYING YOUR
COLLEGE DAYS

FIREWORKS FORTHCOMING

When most people reminisce about their college experience, they will say some variation of "it was the best time of my life." Another common response: "I met my best friends in college," or "It's where I met the love of my life."

While these things might be true — it sure sets a high bar. If you think that you walk onto campus and a little party fairy will descend upon you with umbrella cocktails and insta-friends, you're going to be disappointed.

Starting a new chapter is hard and lonely at first. It will take a while to warm up to your new life, friends, schoolwork, and routines. Be patient and ignore your self-doubt. Understand that most people feel like you, but they're too embarrassed to admit it.

40-year-old you will say "it was the best time of my life," but give the now you a little grace. Fireworks forthcoming.

FRIEND BUFFET

"I wish I would have made the effort to make friends my freshman year. I didn't take advantage of living in the dorms and getting to know lots of different people and it's the one thing I would change if I could do it all over again. Freshman year is the time to meet new people because it gets much harder as time goes by."
Taylor Turner
University of Tennessee

The first few months of Freshman year are like a Friend Buffet: All the chafing dishes are heaped full of food. There's no lack of variety or options. New and interesting flavors and smells everywhere. Servers are directing you where to go, wiping up spills, and refilling trays. Everyone has plenty of time to sit down, relax and enjoy their meal. People are excited and hungry and hopeful. No seats have been claimed yet. It's all a blank cafeteria canvas. Just grab a plate, bon appetit!

As time goes on, the Friend Buffet starts to get picked over. The food has been sitting out and you have to spear through the top layer of funk on the mac 'n cheese. Fewer seats are left to sit and enjoy the meal, as people have either rushed off to their lives or laid claim to seats.

But that's not even the worst of it: the freakin' taco bar station is shut down.

You came late to the Friend Buffet. Mother hell.

Your Freshman year on campus is your chance to be first in line at the Friend Buffet. The first few months at school is when it's easiest to meet new people and make connections. Embrace the awkward, go to the cheesy welcome events, and put yourself out there. Get uncomfortable, you'll thank yourself later.

As time goes on, it will be harder and harder to make new friends as people settle into college life. People will get busy with school work and jobs, some will rush sororities, and leases will be signed for sophomore year apartments.

If you are arriving on campus with friends, explain to them that you want to expand your circle and that they should do the same.

My high school friend wanted to room with me in college. As tempting as it sounded to stick with a sure thing, I knew this was a bad idea. Not because she wouldn't make a good roommate but because I didn't want to live High School, Part Two.

Too chickenshit to have a real conversation with her, and in an attempt to salvage our friendship, I blamed the Michigan State Housing Department for messing up our room assignments and secretly asked them to switch me out of her room.

At first, the joke was on me. My random roomie did not know how to light a candle or make her own bed. Literally. No exaggeration. I'll just leave the rest up to your imagination. (If you're imagining her mom coming to our dorm every weekend to do her laundry and sit awkwardly on our futon making cooing noises for hours — you guessed right!)

However, avoiding my roommate meant that I spent more time getting to know new people. In those first few crucial months, I escaped our room and made friends up and down the hallway.

Probably the most important thing you bring to your dorm room will be a doorstop. Prop your door open and set a precedent in your hallway. Invite people in, peek in other people's rooms, blare your music, and rally the troops on your way to the cafeteria.

Show up early to Friend Buffet and find your people while there's still steam on the taco bar.

"The most important things you'll bring to college are guts and a doorstop."

Kate Hickey

BEFRIEND YOUR ADVISOR

"Advising is so much more than one may think. The relationship built with an Academic Adviser, and allowing them to be your 'go-to person' on campus, helps alleviate a lot of stress and anxiety by just simply knowing someone has your back and is there to support and encourage you every step of the way."
Debbie Lengyel
Director of Advising
Oakland University

Friendly reminder that you are paying a LOT of money to go to school. To uncover all of the ways to maximize your college investment — find a good advisor. If you don't feel like you're vibing with your advisor and they aren't working hard enough for you, request another one and keep emailing and calling until you've found someone who will be a bulldog on your behalf. An advisor is at the school to help you:

- Plan your classes so you can maximize and *strategize* your credits
- Help you with financial aid
- Offer and help you apply for scholarships
- Direct you to study abroad programs and scholarships
- Help you find employment during and after college
- Talk to you about changing majors and the implications of

making the switch
- Direct you in finding answers to questions around your mental health, on-campus activities, and with anything else you need

A good advisor will hook you up and think about your classes strategically. For example, did you know that graduating with a double major or adding a minor does not necessarily mean more work? It's more of a "double dip" of classes and here's how it works:

Take a *History of Latin America* class and it can count toward your history prerequisite AND a major in Spanish AND even a minor in Latin American Studies. Triple dip! One class can fill a requirement for three different programs. If you plan out classes and discuss with your advisor, you can maximize your classes and your money.

Find a great advisor during your freshman year so you can establish this relationship and start off on the right track. They will likely not reach out, so be proactive and get appointments with them on your calendar every semester. Email them with any questions.

If you don't believe this is important, let me tell you that my college advisor is why I now live in Spain. Here's how that played out:

I tell my advisor I want to study abroad but I'm broke → she shows me scholarships → I win one for $500 which covers jack sh*t → I tell her I need more money → she hooks me up with a job on campus → I get money and go to Spain for a summer semester → I have a blast and decide to return when I'm older → I do that.

My advisor also selected me for two leadership opportunities on campus that looked great on my resume and she wrote a reference letter that landed me my first internship.

Use your advisor. Save their number in your phone. Bring

them a plant for their office and a handwritten thank you note. Keep in touch with them after graduation. This is a valuable relationship that most people do not capitalize on. You are not "most people."

PROFESSOR PICKY

If you hate the teacher, you hate the class. That was true in high school, and is no different in college. While you might not always have the option to choose between professors, when you do have an option, do your research.

Check out the website RateMyProfessor.com. This site has student ratings of professors from colleges all over the country. Students give insights into how the class is taught, if class participation makes a big difference in your grade, if they curve, how many exams per course, if they're funny, and more.

Don't look for the easiest classes. Think of blowoff high school classes. You were likely bored, you didn't respect the teacher, and you didn't grow. Essentially, you sat in a chair and played the game in exchange for a number. If you're doing college right — the game has changed.

It's worth the effort to put in a little research and build your schedule around good professors. Ask classmates, your advisor, and upperclassmen to tell you their favorite professor(s). A good professor can make the difference in your grades, desire to go to class, and your interest in the subject area. A great professor can help solidify your passion and career trajectory.

YOUR MAJOR IS NOT THAT MAJOR

If you are feeling pressure to pick the perfect major that will direct your professional trajectory for the rest of your life, please relax.

Most career paths have multiple chapters that are often completely unrelated. We are always changing and growing, learning and pivoting.

According to a study by the Institute of the Future, 85% of jobs that will exist in 2030 haven't been invented yet ("The Next Era"). That means that your degree is not preparing you for the future, it's allowing you to shape the future.

You won't go wrong if you choose something that you are passionate about and that interests you right now. The best way to solve problems that are yet to exist is through pure passion and genuine desire.

Life is not linear. Picture your future as a plot of map dots instead of a straight line. Choosing a major is just one map dot of thousands in your non-linear life.

"I wish everyone would
just tell each other:
'I don't know what I'm
f*cking doing either.'"

GEN ED AND COMMUNITY COLLEGE

*"There's a false pretense that taking Gen Ed courses will help you find out what you want to do. For me, it was about finding out what I didn't like. Instead, I focused on making relationships with people and professors in those prerequisite classes.
Those same people taught higher-level courses
and ended up helping me out immensely."*
Katie Hickman
University of Tennessee

As a Journalism major, I could not wait to sit behind the anchor desk and banter with my makeup artist in between takes of hard-hitting news.

In four years of college I never saw a news camera, much less an anchor desk.

If you are excited to learn all about your career path and eager to learn with other enthusiasts in your field — pump the brakes. Unfortunately, your first two years of college will be basic courses that don't delve into the practical bits of your career.

With that in mind, don't discount local community colleges. They get a bad rap as being the 13th grade but a lot of fabulous professors teach in community colleges. If you are looking to save money, take classes at a community college. You'll be pleasantly surprised at the quality of the content and the savings.

Use your first few semesters to figure out how to be a successful college student. Learn how to study, how to show up to classes you don't love, utilize study groups, and to navigate this new world. It will feel like a slightly harder high school for a while, so stay patient. Junior and senior years open up to more of the exciting and narrowly-focused content, so use the first few semesters in the minor leagues as practice for the majors.

"Do what you have to do so you can do what you want to do."

Oprah Winfrey

PRO TIP: BOOKS

College textbooks are expensive. You will pay the highest book prices at the campus bookstore, so here are a few ways to avoid it:

- Get the book titles or ISBN numbers for your textbooks as soon as possible so you have time to look for deals and cross-shop.
- Your school likely has a Facebook Marketplace you can join to shop for used books.
- Check Library Genesis online. Free PDF downloads are available for some books.
- Websites that sell and buy back college textbooks: Ebay, BigWords.com, CampusBooks.com, Amazon, and more.
- You can rent textbooks too. Chegg.com dominates this space and even offers 21 days to return your book, as well as a study guide and homework assistant service.
- Sometimes your school library has textbooks that can be checked out for the semester. You'll have to renew the book but it will be free.99!
- Share a book or an ebook download with a roommate or classmate.
- Reach out to an upperclassman you trust or check forums to find out if the book is actually used in the class. Nothing is more annoying than spending $80 for a book you crack open once.

- Do a price comparison of major textbook sellers at SlugBooks.com and see who's selling your book at the best price
- Sell your books back! If one website or bookstore won't buy your book back, sell it on Facebook Marketplace or one of the websites listed above.

BACK TO BACK

Everyone says not to take early classes, but that's not the move. The trick is back-to-back classes with few breaks. If you take classes in one big chunk, you will be less likely to skip a class.

Let's play out a schedule that might sound appealing, but is actually not the most efficient use of your time:

10:00am — 11:00am CLASS 1
Your next class starts at 1:00pm. What to do with the next two hours? Eat lunch probably. Doesn't make sense to go to the library and dig in on studying because you'll only have less than an hour with transit time. Can't schedule a work shift or a workout in this window of time either. Maybe just play on your phone and eat. Not much time for anything else.

1:00pm — 2:00pm CLASS 2
Go home, and fall asleep, next class isn't for another three hours. Oops, you overslept. No prob, you'll just be 10 minutes late. Check your phone. Everyone's going out to eat soooo screw it, skip class 3.

5:00pm — 6:00pm CLASS 3
So three classes were spread out from 10am — 6pm. You didn't get up super early but your **entire** day was spent in "school mode." Big gaps between classes are hard to fill with

productivity. Those transit times end up being where you spend money, play on your phone, and idly wait.

The ideal schedule is 9am — 2pm. Back to back classes, no breaks, and be done. The rest of the day is now all yours.

TIME MANAGEMENT

"In high school we were handed our school planners but no one used them. In college, I find my calendar is key to not falling behind. Every month I fill it out with assignments and tests so I know what needs to get done every day."
Dalton Fisher
University of Tennessee

In researching to write this book, the most recurring piece of advice that college students would give to incoming freshmen was to learn how to manage their time. Almost every college student I interviewed said the difference between successful and unsuccessful college students was the ones who knew how to use their time wisely.

In high school, the scheduling was done for you. Teachers reminded you about upcoming tests and you had friends in class that snapped pics of their study guide when you forgot yours. School started every day at the same time, a bell told you to eat, and your parents screamed until you got up. The onus was shared. There was a system and a safety net.

Now you need to create this same machine for yourself. The most useful and practical way to do this is to keep a calendar.

A digital calendar with push notifications or a written calendar will help ensure that you never miss a deadline. Post a calendar with your class schedule somewhere for your roommates. It's nice to know who is home, who's stressed with a big upcoming final, who's hormonal, and who is in class and can't answer their phone.

Think of a calendar as a way of communicating with others and an organizational and educational survival tool.

Time is your most precious commodity and when you physically see your time in an organized system you will be amazed at how well you can use it. If you don't have a system and a routine, being productive will be extremely difficult.

Labeling and updating your calendar is imperative. Below are some best practices that you can incorporate into your calendar flow:

- When professors give you test dates and paper deadlines — put them all in your calendar at the beginning of the course. Now you will be able to see the days you have "free" and weeks that will be hell.
- Block off all of your class times
- Budget and schedule study times ahead of each test or paper
- Budget and schedule exercise
- Share your calendar with your family and close friends if you think it's a fit for you. You don't need your mom to pester you about your upcoming paper, if that's her style, but you might want your roommate to know when you'll be coming and going.
- A calendar will make scheduling work shifts at your job much more manageable too. Input these in your calendar.
- A calendar is for work and play. When you buy tickets to a show — immediately enter them into your calendar. Home game days important to you? Calendar.
- If you want to block off chill time once per week — schedule it and then don't feel guilty about relaxing because you know that you have the time. Read that again. Schedule the mental hygiene time and then take it guilt-free. You need it

and you budgeted for it.

The professional world lives by calendars for a reason. The quicker you can learn to use these digital tools, the better prepared you are. Time and money are stressful when you don't have systems to manage them.

"Let me check my calendar" should be something you say almost daily.

TINY TASKS

Instead of focusing on a lofty goal — concentrate on taking small steps. Big tasks like "finding an internship" can feel daunting, so break the big task into smaller chunks that are more doable. Example:

- January — find three internship opportunities that look interesting
- February — send applications to the three internship opportunities and request to "connect" with stakeholders from each company on LinkedIn
- March — make appointment with my advisor about internship opportunities and follow up with internship applications via email and phone
- April — start over if I don't have an internship or pivot to volunteering

Big to-dos are overwhelming and can have you feeling stressed and hating yourself for not completing them.

Working in micro-tasks brings a sense of accomplishment. Enjoy that little shot of serotonin when something gets crossed off your list because forward momentum feels good. Little milestones are the move.

COLLEGE CARES

Middle school teachers: *"High school teachers will not accept this!"*
High school teachers: *A-*
High School teachers: *"Your college professors won't care."*
College Professors: *"Just stop by during my office hours. I'm happy to help."*

There's a misconception that you are just a number in college and that professors don't care about you or your grades. For the most part, this is completely untrue. Your professors want you to do well. If you work to create a relationship and communicate with them effectively, you will be met with empathy.

Establish a relationship early on. Introduce yourself and visit during office hours to ask questions or to have them review a paper before it's due. Come to class early, or stay a little late and chat. Get off your phone in class because yes, they see you.

When you need a letter of recommendation or some grace on a deadline, professors will be willing to help you because they have gotten to know you as a dedicated student and person.

A little effort on your part will go a long way. Show them you care and they will reciprocate.

THE DEVIL IS IN THE DETAILS

"Read the f*cking syllabus."
Matthew McConn, Associate Professor
Binghamton University

College professors spend a lot of time putting their heart, soul, and blood type into their 9pt font syllabus. It's everything they want you to do: how they want the paper formatted, due dates, office hours...everything.

Extract all the important tests and paper due dates and put them in your calendar at the beginning of the semester. Save the syllabus on your desktop and reference it before you ask any dumbass questions or turn in any assignment. Read the syllabus.

"College be like:
You: Hey Professor how
you doing today?
Professor: It's on the syllabus."
Malik Green

PAPER AND PROFESSOR POINTERS

You will be writing and reading a lot. Here are a few fast tips from college professors to help you write at the college level:

Space Sucking Sucks

It is often interesting and so very typical for the majority of these groups, in my opinion, and for the ...

Re-read that sentence. Do you notice how it's just words going nowhere? It's space-sucking, BS, made-up-crap, or rambling and it's very transparent.

At the college level, give up the word count tricks, margin scooting, paragraph indenting, and whatever other get-me-to-six-pages-moves you're trying to pull. Professors see this for what it is. Get to your point, back it up with examples, justify it with the text, and/or cite sources.

If you ramble too much in your writing or emails, you will appear unsure of yourself. You'll hit the word count but miss the grade.

Re-Read the Assignment

Did you answer the question asked of you in the assignment? Reread the rubric, syllabus, or prompt and make sure that you addressed the problem or answered the question clearly. It's simple and overlooked, but always make your point clear.

Demonstrate You've Read or Paid Attention in Class
Reference your notes from class, and interject points the professor or colleagues have made during lectures. This shows that you are invested in the material and professors will take note. Same with assigned reading.

Excessive Exclamation!!!!
At the college level and beyond, excessive exclamation is a cheap concealer for bad writing. If you want your audience to feel — use words, not punctuation.

Exclamation points are the grammatical equivalent of someone telling you to smile. Piss off. We can't expect our readers to be excited all the time and I refuse to force excitement when it's likely a Monday and the best thing that happened to me today was eating a hoagie.

Same goes for all caps and bold text. Over-excited grammar reads juvenile. Be thrilling with adjectives and evidence.

EMAIL IS EVERYTHING

Emails are your ticket to success and building key relationships. Harness the power of crafting a good email and opportunities will present themselves.

It's considered sloppy to omit capitalization and to use abbreviations or shorthand. Always include a subject that includes your full name and course, and make sure to use an introduction and greeting. Example:

Subject: Milo Herring: History 440 M/W/F Class

Hello Professor McShmessor,

My name is Milo Herring and I am a freshman student in your M/W/F History 440 class. I am writing to let you know that the online portal would not allow the submission for my paper after I tried several times from three different internet browsers. I am attaching the paper to this email titled "Milo Herring: End of Era" and I apologize for the inconvenience and appreciate your understanding in the matter. Should you need me to resubmit, I am happy to do so but wanted to ensure that my paper would be turned in on time. I am also happy to deliver a printed copy to your office if that works with your schedule.

Thank you for your time and enjoy your weekend,

Milo Herring

I mean, what grade would you give this kid?

Prof. McSchmessor I tried to turn my paper in but its not working. I'm sending it to u in an email so its not late. So sorry I literally tried a million times! Thx so much!!...Milo

First of all with the exclamation points, I can't. Second, literally is so misused I literally want to slap someone.

Professors have hundreds of students each year and employers have thousands of emails and balls to juggle. Always clarify exactly who you are, what you're asking, and do not skip the intro and outro niceties.

Remember also that professors are not your IT support so if you have problems with attachments or the class online forum, don't ask them for help. They teach content, so you need to figure that out on your own. Another way to piss off your professor, tell them you're "super busy." Bad move.

Reread your email before you hit send. Check for tone and typos.

Most jobs are promoting and hiring good communication skills. With good email etiquette you can do anything. Without it, you're literally screwed!!!!

CREATE CONNECTIONS IN CLASS

On the first week of school, find someone in each of your classes, sit down and immediately say hey. Ask if you can exchange contact info in case either of you ever needs anything from class. Text them immediately and save their number under the name of the class and their name.

Everyone knows this is the move, and they will secretly be relieved you had the guts to ask so they didn't have to ask. Connections in classes matter because you will get sick, miss class, or forget something important that the professor said.

"Anthony History210" might save your ass when you decide at the last minute to stay that extra night on your Miami spring break trip.

STUDYING VS. STUDYING

I'm guilty of skipping a couple of burpees to fix my ponytail, or omitting that last push up because I "had" to have a sip of water or I'd die. Loose shoelaces, bathroom breaks — you know all the exercise avoidance moves. You're still working out though, right? Yeahhhh.

Similarly, there are two types of studying: Actively taking on information and retaining it and *playing the part* of someone studying. The faster you can learn to stop telling yourself you're studying and get to work, the more free time you'll have.

All of the study prep makes you feel like you are doing what you should, but it's really just delaying the inevitable. Getting dressed and packed, buying a fun caffeinated drink, walking to a special study spot, coordinating with friends, stopping short because you need to change your laundry (subconsciously you wanted an excuse to bail anyway) are all of the "I'm studying" ways to tell yourself you're studying. Yeahhhh.

There's nothing wrong with ritualizing study time, finding a great study spot or drink that energizes you. However, you've got to actually trust yourself to sit down and get the work done. Put your phone away, stop skimming the pages, don't allow distractions, and actually put in the work. Spend some good focused time and be done.

Ultimately, mastering smart study habits means mastering your time, focusing your energy, staying true to your promises to yourself, and maintaining a low-stress level.

All of these tricks you use to tell yourself you're studying are the equivalent of fixing your shoelaces in a workout. You're expending the wrong kind of energy and nothing is actually getting done. Do the damn burpee.

Study Tips:

1. Know how you learn and retain information.
Do you learn by seeing? By hearing something? By doing it yourself? For me, I can't just highlight in the book (that's just turning words from confusing in black and white to confusing in yellow and black). I have to draw little pictures and sketches in the margins or explain a complicated concept to someone else in my own words. If you know *how* you learn, you will be able to help reinforce and solidify the learning for yourself.

2. Reading is not studying.
Just because you read a manual on how to fly a plane doesn't mean I'm getting on a plane with you. Reading is the pre-work. Now you need to *understand* the concepts by creating a diagram, timeline, or creating a quiz for yourself.

3. Find a documentary or TED talk on the topic.
Adding something visual to your learning will help you to understand it at a deeper level. The documentary, YouTube video, or TED talk might not be exactly in sync with your learning but it will help you understand concepts in a more captivating and memorable way.

4. Stop the Distractions.

Every interruption costs you time and energy to refocus. If you can't stay off your phone, download an app like *SelfControl* that blocks specific websites or social media for your desired amount of time. Every time you "change gears" while doing something, it takes 15 minutes to regain focus. Stay dialed in and get the job done.

"When relatives say 'Sure looks
like you're having a lot
of fun in college.'
Yeah Tina I don't post pics of
me crying in the library."

OWN YOUR WORK STYLE

Figure out how you best work and then embrace it. Procrastinators get a bad wrap, but people who work quickly under pressure, or tight deadlines, are assets in the workforce. If you are more structured with your studies, this preparedness is a great strength.

If you can wait until the day before to crank out a paper, starting at midnight half-buzzed after a concert, just do that. If you need a five-day lead time, plan for it.

Whatever your style is, own it.

Procrastinators — don't beat yourself up all weekend and stress about a paper due on Monday when you know in your late 'lil heart that you're going to write it all on Sunday night. Enjoy your weekend and relax. Your strengths are revealed in the fourth quarter.

Methodical students — set aside one hour every day to write and budget for it on your calendar. You know the final hour makes you anxious so daily progress will keep you feeling productive and in control of the assignment.

Understanding how you work best will mean that you can enjoy the time when you're not working, instead of being all-consumed by all the things. Your work style is as fixed as your eye color. Work accordingly.

OWN YOUR GRADES

True story: A hardworking college freshman received a 50% on a paper they had worked on tirelessly. Confused and discouraged, they went to ask the professor how to improve the grade and find out what they could do differently for the subsequent assignments to help raise their overall grade in the course.

The professor responded to that email with something like: "This paper is fantastic! An absolute A and exactly the analysis I was looking for. I am so sorry for any confusion, but my Teacher Assistant graded this paper and I did not read it until you brought it to my attention. I will speak with my TA and amend your grade immediately."

If you're thinking WTF — you should be. Humans make errors. Computers make errors. I can't tell you how many times I entered double zeros in my grade book as a teacher when I meant to enter a 100.

Make a habit of checking up on any grades that you don't understand. Do this without being defensive but with the intention of understanding the grade and how you can improve moving forward.

Maybe the analysis was great, but the formatting or bibliography was the problem. Your professor might be up for letting you rewrite or re-submit. You'll never know unless you ask. In asking, you are forging a relationship with this person and they will see that you are a serious, communicative, and committed person.

Offer to come in during office hours to discuss, and remember that you are the customer. You are paying a lot of money for a college degree and you should make inquiries about your work.

YOU BROKE

*"Use the dining hall, you only get it for one year and you'll miss
the experience. Also, your budget is not everyone
else's so don't try to live like it is."*
Addie Fisher
University of Tennessee Knoxville

Get prepared to spend most of your 20s broke. While it's not
ideal, this financial bootcamp is both great training for life and
a right of passage.

- Get organized. Write down all of your incoming and
  outgoing expenditures — understand where you can cut
  costs and where you're spending in excess. There are dozens
  of apps for this.
- Get comfortable talking to others about your financial
  reality. "I can't go out to eat, I don't have the money" or
  "Thanks for the invite, but I don't get paid until Friday."
  Your real friends will appreciate the honesty and eat grilled
  cheese with you at home.
- No beer or burrito is worth an overdraft fee of $39.
- Face the music. Don't let anything pile up or you'll be
  facing late payment charges and reinstatement fees. Open
  the email or check the banking app but do not avoid your
  financial reality because you feel overwhelmed or saddened

by it. Ignoring your finances will only exacerbate the problem and delay the inevitable.

- Make calls. You are the customer for your loans, car payments, insurance, and credit cards. Call up the customer service department and explain your need for an extension, to skip a month's payment, or ask to lower your interest rates. You'll be surprised that most companies offer a little wiggle room for you if you just take the time to ask. Be assertive and sugary-sweet and if you get a no, call back.
- Be careful on the weekends with *Venmo* as most transactions don't process or deposit until Monday.
- Set goals. Being broke doesn't mean saving is impossible. Set a goal and stick to it. You won't miss that pair of shoes you didn't buy when you're eating a croissant at a bakery in Paris. It will just taste sweeter because you saved and paid for it.

Money, or lack thereof, does not have to rule your life. Own your financial reality and your budget.

For now, you broke.

STUDENT DISCOUNTS

Your student ID can save you a lot of money. Pull out that bad boy everywhere and ask in your best "help me, I'm poor" voice.

Student discounts are always changing and often, even the cashiers might not be aware that their store offers a student discount so get in the habit of asking. Discounts also vary by location. In general, most people have a heart for college kids and will hook you up. Below is a list of great discounts. For an updated guide go to collegeinfogeek.com (2021).

Technology:

- Spotify+Hulu+Showtime for $4.99/month if you sign up with your .edu email
- Apple Music for only 4.99/month if you sign up with your .edu email
- Adobe — save 70% on Creative Cloud
- Lenovo — 5%

Clothing

- Levi's — 15%
- Banana Republic — 15%

- Kate Spade — 15%
- J. Crew — 15%
- Madewell — 15%
- Steve Madden — 10%
- Topshop — 10%

Food

- *Most of these vary by location but it can't hurt to ask
- Arby's — 10%
- Buffalo Wild Wings — 10%
- Burger King — 10%
- Chick-fil-a — free drink
- Chipotle — free drink
- Dunkin Donuts — 10%
- McDonald's — 10%
- Pizza Hut — 10%
- Qdoba — free drink
- Subway — 10%

Other

- Amazon Student — 50% off Amazon Prime and free two-day shipping
- Amtrak Train Tickets — 15% off
- Greyhound Bus — 20% with a student advantage card
- FedEx — 20-30% off shipping prices
- NYTimes — one month free and $1/week if you sign up with your .edu email

For getting good grades, insurance companies like Allstate, Nationwide, and Progressive offer car insurance discounts. If you use your school email, cell phone providers like Sprint and AT&T also offer student discounts. Never hurts to ask.

FIND ME IN THE CLUB

"Get comfortable being uncomfortable. Find a mentor, join a club, attend events, and be engaged in campus life. Experiences will shape you, your connections, and your future."
Seneca Wilson
Mississippi State University

Sophomore year, I joined the Michigan State Outing Club. It was initially because I liked the t-shirts and went through a short-lived "outdoor bro" phase, but this accident turned out to be the move.

The Outing Club put together rafting trips, kayaking excursions, skydiving dates, and rock climbing trips. No experience required.

So I bought my fancy Nalgene water bottle and started a collection of eclectic stickers from brands I couldn't afford or pronounce. I was trying on the outdoors like a basic bitch, but the keyword was "trying" so that's something!

It was a great way to meet a new group of diverse and chill people and to try things I'd never done. Everything from the carpooling and camping gear to the kegs and campfire coffee was organized for us at a deeply discounted group rate.

I went whitewater rafting in West Virginia while the fall leaves were changing color and it was incredible. I kayaked during the salmon run while two-foot-long fish slapped my oar — unforgettable experiences that I would not have done without the Outing Club.

There are hundreds and sometimes thousands of student organizations at most universities: intramural sports (co-ed or single-gender), gay choir, acro-yoga, Pre-Pharmacy Club, African Empowerment, Criminal Justice, Ballroom Dancing, Birding, Bikram, and Birdwatching — just to name a few.

Search the online list of student organizations at your school and go to a few meetings of any club that looks interesting to you. If you can't find what you're looking for, then start a club. How awesome would that look on your LinkedIn profile?

Be brave and go to the meeting alone so that you are pushed to make a new friend.

Plus free shirts...and food!

FREEDOM OF ANONYMITY

No one cares what you look like in class or at the cafeteria. You might spend a whole day on campus and see one person you know by name. This anonymity is gloriously freeing. Brush your teeth and take the occasional shower...anything beyond is just a bonus. Plus, you can wear the same thing two days in a row because your Monday, Wednesday, and Friday people don't know about your Tuesday and Thursday life.

You will likely have two college looks: Dirtbag McGee and Glowed TF Up. There will be no in-between.

If you've come to impress with labels and looks — it's because you enjoy those things. No one else will notice or care. Pack less than you think you need and save your money and energy.

DON'T GO HOME EVERY WEEKEND

You will be tempted to go back to the comforts of home and the familiar. If you are lucky, you have parents who are eager to spoil you, cook for you, and do your laundry. Try to avoid this temptation. If you keep going back, you can't go forward.

When you go home, you're the hero. Everyone misses you, the pantry is full and the family dog is somehow cuter than when you last left. Free food, free gas, and all the familiar creature comforts.

Don't forget all the "shopping" you'll do around the house before you go back. By shopping, I mean stealing toilet paper, loose quarters, and anything that's not nailed down.

Those are the perks of going home, but the drawbacks are important to think through too.

You can't get a college experience at your childhood home.

I'm not saying skip the holidays, but keep the novelty of going home as just that: a novelty, not a place of refuge.

Things are going to get tough, awkward, uncomfortable, and boring at school. Try to stick it out.

If you are going home to avoid any of these feelings, you need to reevaluate how you cope with these challenges and ask yourself, "Is going home allowing me to grow? Am I just scared? Bored? Broke?"

If you're going home because you're broke — you might as

well move back in. Your ass is going to be broke for at least the next four years. Get used to it.

YOUR FIRST SUMMER HOME

After living a life of doing whatever/whenever at school, it's a big transition to be back at home. A full year of drinking without judgment, late nights, and clothes strewn wherever they land — it's hard to return to a home that feels like a stifled version of the new you.

With our parents we want it both ways — to be a child (help me I'm poor, love me, be proud of me, find my charger, my tire needs air) but we also want to be adults (it doesn't matter what time I'm home, it's my money, don't worry I'll handle it). This is a hard balance to strike and it takes a lot of patience from both parties.

Just remember, you are now a guest. Possibly your parents are paying for you to live at school *and* giving you a free summer home.

While you've been away, they have lived another life without you, so have a heart when you come waltzing back in with all your crap and expectations of continuing your college life in your childhood home. This is an adjustment for them too.

Help out, be respectful of the house rules, and understand that you are sharing a space with your most favorite and loving people. They were the ones that moved all your stuff, Venmoed you, listened to your whining, and never complained. These were the people you called all year when you were at your lowest lows. They deserve you at your best.

Before you get home, communicate about expectations. Ask

for clear ground rules: An agreed-upon curfew, chores, work schedules, meal times, etc. You've lived with a roommate so you know how it feels when people are inconsiderate or don't pull their weight.

Be a good roommate. These are your people.

YOU GET TO

If college was a given for you — that's amazing and you don't need to feel any way about that. Treat your privilege with gratitude and hug your parents or grandparents. If you're working to put yourself through school — you're my hero. If you're a mix — awesome.

But if you need a reality check, watch an inner-city kid delivering pizzas bawl his eyes out when Ellen surprises him with an oversized $25,000 scholarship check from Shutterfly. Puts things in real perspective.

If you're in the negativity spiral of "I have to go to class" or "I have to write this seven-page paper by Thursday," try changing just one word in this sentence, and instead of "have to," use "get to," and see if it alters your mindset.

I get to go to class. I get to learn skills that will land me a good job. I get to go to the library. I get to spend time building a successful future for myself. I get to spend four years investing and developing myself as a person.

College is an opportunity to change the trajectory of your life and it's easy to forget this in the daily grind. You *get to* go to college. Lucky you.

PART THREE

ON BUILDING YOUR CAREER

YOUR GRADES DON'T MATTER THAT MUCH

"I just graduated but if I could relive college I would tell myself to chill out. I didn't need to be so anxious and stressed out about my grades and so many other inconsequential things."
Conner Barnett
Chattanooga State

Companies hire experience, attitude, and work ethic. Period.

As a business owner, I was charged with reviewing resumes and hiring. The first thing I did after receiving a resume was a nice long Instagram stalking session followed by a little LinkedIn tour. I completely ignored grades, Dean's Lists, and BlahCumLaude and jumped straight to: what can this candidate *do*? Do their actions show *ambition and drive*? Will they understand our customers? Can they get things done without me holding their hand? Do they seem optimistic and professional?

These are all things that can only be demonstrated with experience, not with tests.

Set yourself up for post-grad success and get an internship. Volunteer for a company you're interested in, shadow jobs, and get real-world experience.

While it's tempting to go back to your Olive Garden job at

home during the summers, push yourself to get experience in your field. Do both if you need money and a beefier resume.

If you have to choose between getting an A or B on a paper and turning in three internship applications, or study abroad scholarships, choose the latter. Grades don't matter as much as experience.

"Our greatest fear should not be of failure, but of succeeding at life in things that don't really matter."

Francis Chan

FINDING A JOB IS A JOB

Finding a job after college is a full-time job. Same with a summer or post-graduate internship. It's a lot of work and time to research companies, prep a resume, email cover letters, follow up, and stalk the internet.

The process is soul-sucking. It's going to bed dejected, to wake up and get kicked straight in the genitals, day after day.

I wish there was a silver bullet or even a morsel of wisdom that could make this an easier pill to swallow. Unfortunately, it just sucks. If job or internship-hunting feels difficult and hopeless and seems to take up your entire life — you are doing it right. If you need to work part-time at Old Navy to make ends meet while you job hunt, there is absolutely nothing wrong with that.

Here are some down and dirty "new job" tips:

- When you are interviewing, remember that these are the people you will be spending the majority of your time with. Do they seem kind, fun, interesting, and team-oriented? You are vetting them as much as they are you.
- Research the company before you consider it. Stalk the employees online and see what you uncover about the vision, goals, and overall vibe. Reference specifics from your search in the interview and use their language.

- There's a fine line between paying your dues as the new person and acting small. Do not feel like your age is a reason to be treated as a second-class citizen. You were hired for your potential and to show them your potential, you'll have to speak up sometimes.
- Your resume should be one page with clickable URLs to work examples and/or your LinkedIn profile. And, for the love of Pete, convert the file to a PDF.
- Invest in quality clothing. If you only have a closet full of oversized hoodies and jeans that look like you got attacked by a shark, your first few paychecks will be spent on looking like a grown up. Think chic and timeless.
- Try not to take rejection or feedback personally.
- If you don't know how to do something, Google it.
- Do not be intimidated by anyone or any task.
- Everyone in your job matters. Your next move will most likely depend on the connections you make in your current job. Learn from *everyone*. Some of my most insightful conversations and relationships were with janitors.

Stay patient. No job is permanent nor perfect. You got this. In the meantime, remember that being unemployed is not a reflection of your self-worth.

GET OUTTA TOWN

"I was an over-thinking introvert when I first studied abroad in London. I was dreading being in a group setting and terrified at the idea of depending on others and admitting I was a beginner traveler. However, I discovered a confident, capable, and assertive side of myself. It's been such an empowering experience."
Makala Marsee
Lipscomb University

If confidence were a pie chart, I'd say 10% of my courage is genes, 30% was learned through failure, and 60% of my conviction comes from living and traveling abroad.

Until you experience it for yourself, a trip abroad appears to be about the sights, the photos, and the exotic locations themselves. The reality is that it's all about the inner journey.

Travel is learning on steroids. It's navigating an airport for the first time alone, talking to a cabbie in nods and broken Chinese to find your way back to your hotel, conversations over beers with strangers, and figuring out how to buy a subway ticket with foreign coins.

Travel pushes you into places of yourself you never knew were there and it pulls the "I got this" file from way back in your brain and puts it to work every day to show you can do anything.

To take a trip or spend a semester abroad, you do not have to be rich — just determined and resourceful. Here are some great ways to get abroad:

- **Study abroad** — talk to your advisor for scholarships and ask professors for advice. Most study abroad programs offer the same few courses year after year in the same destination. If you know in advance that your preferred program/destination offers specific classes, make sure you don't take those courses on campus. "Save" them for your study abroad program and you won't waste time and money on credits that don't apply to your major. If you budget right, a summer abroad can be as affordable as a summer on campus.
- **Become a pet/house/farm sitter** — There are dozens of websites that connect pet sitters and pet owners all over the globe. Build a profile on a few of these platforms and go take care of someone's house or small farm in exchange for a free stay.
- **Au pair** — Families abroad are always looking for trusted babysitters for their children that are also native English speakers. As an au pair, you live with a family and care for their children. You also get to go on their vacations with them and receive a small payment as well as nights/weekends off to go out and explore. Living with a family has its perks because they will introduce you to local people and flavors you would never know about otherwise.
- **Intern Abroad** — Many internship abroad programs include traditional housing and meal plans as well as small stipends. These programs are a great way to get experience, connections, and get a few destinations crossed off your bucket list.
- **Volunteer Abroad** — Opportunities span from organic farming to international policy, but be careful with programs that are too costly. Beyond a plane ticket, you shouldn't need to pay for much.

- **Work Exchange** — Again, there are lots of online platforms that do this. In general, you are expected to work around five hours a day in exchange for food and accommodation.
- **Gap Year** — Avoid school burnout and explore what excites you. A gap year can be a semester or a year of volunteer work, travel, or interning and some schools have structured gap year programs that eliminate the guesswork.

Do your homework before you choose a program or company to travel with as they are a business looking to make money. The best way to vet any program is by speaking to someone who has used their services.

Getting yourself abroad will be the first step in your new journey of discovering that your badassness has no limits. You can navigate a new and exciting world on your own. Get on Google, start budgeting, ask for travel money at Christmas and birthdays, set up profiles on a few platforms, get a passport, and find one scholarship. Make it happen.

When you get stuck, remember that if it were easy, everyone would do it. Travel is reserved for those that are willing to go the extra mile. (hehe)

Stow your fears along with your tray table and check your insecurities with your luggage. The plane will be your only descent because your newfound sense of self has taken off and will never land.

The most important souvenir from your travels: the realization that you are your own life jacket and oxygen mask. Wheels up, party peeps.

JUST ASK

I used to watch House Hunters International with my eight-year-old and dream about living abroad. Seeing international cities and watching couples fight while they pick out a home in a foreign country is more entertaining than people watching at an amusement park.

When we finally got the chance to move my family to Spain, I thought — why not apply to be on the show?

Turns out, all you had to do was write an email. I didn't get a response on the first email so I tried again four months later, and got an immediate reply from the casting agent. We filmed the show, and it was a blast. We also became great friends with the film crew and, as a bonus, have a time capsule of an amazing chapter in our lives.

Sometimes when you want something, you just have to ask.

The worst thing that can happen is that you get a no, but don't be afraid to ask. People want to help you — it makes them feel valued and a part of something bigger than themselves.

Reach out via email or stop by their office and be honest and vulnerable. "I've researched your company and feel like I could help you solve _____ problem with my _____ skills. I am a hard worker and a quick learner. Would you be open to a conversation about what I can bring to your company?"

People will really surprise you in a good way.

DON'T TELL, DO

If you can't find a formal internship, invent your own by taking a Khan Academy training online or find someone with your dream job and shadow them. Go collect experiences and, before you know it, your resume will be stacked with skills and proof of your ambition.

Here is just one example of how to do this for an Advertising, Marketing, or Journalism Major:

Offer to take over a social media sales campaign for a semester for a small business that interests you. Watch YouTube tutorials if you run into a speed bump. Keep track of the growth the account gets as a result of your efforts. Offer to write a few blog posts for social and their website. Ask for a small budget to run ads.

The business will love you for doing the work for free, or cheap, and will write you an amazing letter of recommendation and endorse you for all sorts of skills on LinkedIn.

This example works for almost any major as marketing/sales is a great way to understand both client and customer and can be tailored to almost any skillset: photography, graphic design, web development, branding, and fashion merchandising are just a few.

Use this experience to write at least five to six resume lines. Here are a few examples:

1. Grew Lucy's Ice Cream social media following from 933 followers to 2,301 followers and drove 30,500 clicks to their website in five months

2. Increased traffic to Lucy's Ice Cream 4x by writing weekly blog posts optimized for SEO.

3. Increased online sales by 9% through campaign efforts

Internships are just one way to get experience. Be creative in inventing real-world experiences and solving problems. Your ingenuity, in and of itself, will speak volumes to your capabilities and work ethic.

DON'T TAKE NO FOR AN ANSWER

My husband desperately wanted to play for the NBA since he was old enough to dribble a basketball. As a husky 5'6" dude who was only mediocre at basketball, he decided working for the NBA would have to do.

As you can imagine, lots of people want to work in professional sports so he had to be ruthless. There were no advertised internship openings and at age 19, he had really no skills that qualified him to do anything beyond cleaning floors.

After five months of emails, phone calls, and countless voicemails, he finally got a reply:

"Yes, ok come work at *one* game, but we don't pay interns," was the exhausted response.

He worked one game (in the same saggy butt olive green suit we met in) and was given the cold shoulder. There were no available internship positions.

For six more months, he stalked the director of the department and finally got a call back offering him eight hours of work per week. He was tasked with organizing closets and making copies — for zero dollars an hour and for zero college credit.

In a quest to make connections, he went from office to office and asked: "Hi, I'm Paul the intern, is there anything I can help you with?"

Over a few months, he had made himself indispensable by asking, learning, and lurking. Gradually he got more and more responsibilities and was offered a paid position for college credit.

He worked for the NBA for six years, climbing his way up the ladder and finally leaving as the Director of Public Relations with three championship rings and countless stories on private jets and NBA courts all over the world.

Professional people are busy. They are doing a thousand things a day, answering hundreds of emails, and raising their families. While you are fixated on your inbox and waiting for job replies, they are running from meeting to meeting and taking calls in between.

Don't feel like you are pestering employers when you follow up on your application. They are busy and have forgotten about you, and not because you aren't awesome, but because they are juggling a thousand balls.

If you're thinking "I just reached out to them last week. I don't want to be annoying," think again.

From the employer's perspective, an attractive trait is to receive multiple emails and phone calls from a candidate. It shows that you follow through and have passion for their company.

Be brave. You are not a bother.

Just because you're not athletic or seven-feet-tall doesn't mean you can't play in the NBA. Rejection is inevitable. Do not let it stop you.

"The better you are at communicating, negotiating, and handling your fear of rejection, the easier life is."

Robert Kiyosaki

LINKEDIN FOR THE WIN

Of all the social media accounts you have, LinkedIn is the most important. It's not Facebook for old people, it's your online resume and it's where all the employers are.

Here are some tips to maximize your LinkedIn profile:

- Write a great headline and summary statement. Not sure what that looks like? Stalk other profiles.
- Add a "click here to view my LinkedIn profile" to your resume with a link to your LinkedIn page. (Yes the link will still be clickable when you send it as a PDF).
- Include part-time and full-time work, volunteering, unpaid work, and internships and don't be shy — this is your chance to show off what you know and what you can do. If you wonder about adding something, the answer is likely yes.
- Get former managers, teachers, and colleagues to "endorse" your skills and write a review for you.
- Connect with colleagues, family, friends, professors, and anyone you can. If you do not personally know the person, add an introduction line so they know you are not a bot. Some people will not accept cold connection requests.
- Slide into those DMs with inquiries on internships or job opportunities. If you're not sure you've reached the right person, add a line like. "If you are not the appropriate person for this inquiry, I would appreciate you passing my

information to the right person."

- Upload or link your work on your profile. If you are a writer or artist, make LinkedIn your portfolio.
- Connect with people as soon as you meet them to solidify relationships and build your network. If you go to a career fair or an interview, try and connect with as many people as you can on LinkedIn that same day, before they have a chance to forget you. Add a line with your connection request: "I enjoyed meeting you this morning at the recruiting event and I would love to..." Make up a reason to talk to them. Share an interesting article, thank them for their time, etc.
- If you are hoping to work at a specific company, connect with people at that company and intelligently comment on their posts.
- Try to keep connections "warm" by commenting on their posts and DMing them. If you keep in touch online, they will be more likely to be in your corner.
- Want to work in a specific vertical? Share articles and interesting news related to your desired field on your feed and tag company accounts or people. This shows you know what's up and you're passionate.

LinkedIn is not the time to be shy or humble. In the digital world, you can reach out to people in a meaningful way without having to drive or sweat through awkward coffee meet-ups in your cheap blazer. Take advantage of this platform and get the competitive edge.

Choose a professional headshot and start making connections now. The first thing a potential employer will do when they get your resume is go directly to your LinkedIn profile. Wow them when they get there.

IT'S A SMALL WORLD AFTER ALL

When I was 22, I met my fabulous and steadfast friend, Kelly. She has become family to me over our 20-plus years of friendship. Kelly married my husband's best friend, and we are the Godparents to their twins. Her relentless encouragement is a big reason this book is in your hands.

When we first met, Kelly always talked about her "really good high school friend" but only in pronouns — never by name. After almost a year, Kelly finally used the girl's name: Amber.

Yep, you guessed it, *the* Amber I kicked out of the Beta house.

Great. So my inauthenticity is back to haunt me and she's brought her friend Karma.

This isn't a don't-be-mean-or-karma-will-find-you lesson. It's actually a the-world-is-very-small lesson. I thought that the anonymity of 40,000 students at Michigan State would allow me to be a moral-dodging butthole but that too blew up in my face.

This is how life works out. Everyone is connected and these connections matter. They matter professionally and personally — and often they are so intertwined, it's hard to disentangle the two.

Treat people like you will see them again. Speak to them like they will be your child's future teacher. Thank them like they will be your mom's oncologist. Keep in touch with them like they are your future boss.

"Be nice. The world
is a small town."

Austin Kleon

WHAT REALLY MATTERS

Want to know what college graduates have found to be the most valuable benefits from their university degree?

Soft skills. Soft skills are things like managing workload, teamwork, flexibility, leadership, creativity, problem solving, etc.

Over 62% of college students surveyed said that soft skills and personal experiences were the most valuable benefits of their college degree. (Johnson, 2020).

What that means is that work ethic, time management, problem solving, and relationship-building are going to be more beneficial to you than the specific skills you acquire in your degree.

The great news: This is not connected to picking the perfect major or making perfect grades.

This also means that mental hygiene is again worth mentioning. Being a creative, flexible, and organized person can't happen if your mind isn't right.

A DEGREE MIGHT NOT BE FOR ME

I'll spare you the list of famous people who dropped out of college and will get straight to the truth: Today's job market is hiring experience and hard work. While going to college is a worthwhile endeavor for some — it's not a one-size-fits-all solution.

If you make an informed decision and choose to drop out of college, congrats. You have made your first adult decision that is right for you at the time. Now for step two: Never belittle your choice. *"I didn't go to college, but I …"*

No but.

There are plenty of pricks with letters after their names and millions of hairdressers that make a daily difference in people's lives and self-worth. Let go of the stigma that college defines success, and embrace what brings you joy.

Think about the person that means the most to you or who changed your life. Likely it wasn't a neurosurgeon but an aunt or a coach. These are the difference makers and they come in all flavors.

So if you want to drop out of college to protect your mental health, get out of debt, or for any other reason — trust yourself to know what you need. You're not a "drop out," you're an "I-know-what's-best-for me" and those people hold a BA in Happiness and a Ph.D. in Bravery.

"You'll never make good decisions
if you need everyone in your life
to think your decisions are good."
T. Coleman

PERFECT TIMING

Stop putting pressure on yourself with deadlines. You're going to watch friends post their engagement rings and it will make you question your life. You'll see someone buy a house and think "shit, I have $3.42 to my name and I can't even keep a cactus alive." Relax. You have your whole life to craft your life.

In case you need some real-world examples of timing (Moss, 2016):

At age 23, Tina Fey was working at a YMCA.

At age 23, Oprah was fired from her first reporting job.

At age 24, Stephen King was working as a janitor and living in a trailer.

At age 27, Vincent Van Gogh started art school.

At age 28, J.K. Rowling was a suicidal single parent living on welfare.

Vera Wang failed to make the Olympic figure skating team, didn't get the Editor-in-Chief position at Vogue, and designed her first dress at age 40.

Samuel L. Jackson didn't get his first movie role until he was 46.

Let's normalize narratives where friends live together with lots of cats and have relationships that don't involve pink and blue icing or wedding hashtags.

There are a million ways to do life.

Have Fun Be Safe I Love You

"You're not behind in life. There's no timetable that we all must follow. It's made up. Seven billion people can't do the same thing in order. What's early? What's late? Compared to who? Don't beat yourself up for where you are. It's your schedule and everything is right on time."

Emily Maroutian
The Book of Relief

DON'T WAIT FOR FATE

You can be paralyzed by searching for "the perfect opportunity, partner, job, etc" and end up never trying anything because it wasn't *just* right.

Make moves. Don't worry if they're the right ones. Don't question your plan or direction, just move and act.

Along the way, you'll make connections and acquire skills. Don't sit around and wait for fate to drop the perfect anything in your lap. Be afraid, be unsure, and do it anyway.

"If opportunity doesn't knock,
build a door."

Milton Berle

IN THE WEEDS

"Careers aren't picked out of a hat. The best ones are discovered (and change) over time as you gain experience, learn about new ideas and opportunities, and build relationships with interesting people you admire."
Cameron Sorsby

I remember one of my students who almost didn't graduate high school. Pot leaves drawn on his notebooks and a smirk drawn on his face, Alex never had his Spanish work done. He could tell you the THC potency levels in every strain of marijuana but was bombing sophomore science. Alex was failing my class too and driving me nuts.

I told him after class one day: "So let me get this straight, your passion is *weed*? How are you going to make a living then, become a drug dealer? Move to South America and be a weed farmer? Stop wasting my time and your time and do your Spanish homework so you can graduate."

Welp, let me tell you what this little turd did: He moved to South America and grew weed. Actually, that is a *massive* understatement. Alex learned how to cleverly market marijuana during a time when it was heavily regulated. He was making bank, completely above board, and creating connections all over the globe with innovative solutions to an emerging market. By the time marijuana was legalized, Alex was light years ahead of the industry.

He was a passionate young entrepreneur and I was projecting my values onto him.

Recently, on one of his world travels, Alex made a stop in Spain to visit me. We had breakfast and chatted about new marketing strategies he uses and how they could help my business, exchanged travel stories, and memories. He has gone on to design and manufacture sneakers, shoot photography all over the world, run countless ultra-marathons, speak Spanish (maybe my homework wasn't so important after all), and has created a happy and fulfilled life.

Alex turned his passion into a career. He ignored what he was taught about conventional success, status, and stability and followed his interests and intuition.

I wish I would have apologized for my small-mindedness at that breakfast but I know he'll read this and understand. I am so proud of you Alex.

I close this book with his story because your teachers, professors, parents, society, and college are preparing you for a world that doesn't exist.

The training and learning that you're doing right now is going to be outdated quickly, so your attitude, mindset, innovation, work ethic, agility, and empathy are what matter most.

Ignore all of the voices (including your own) that tell you "you can't make a life doing that." With a little resilience and lots of hard work, you can make a life doing absolutely anything, anywhere.

LAST CALL

Well, I'm out. I hope you've learned that you can relax a little. You don't have to have it all figured out. We will never have it all figured out.

Take care of yourself and your thoughts. Trust your instincts, and show yourself a lot of grace.

Be kind, karma has a long memory.

Ask people for help. Play to your strengths. Put your phone down. Try cool stuff and meet as many people as you can.

Remember that you are on your own timeline and journey and anyone who gets in your way or doubts you is not "your people." For the lucky ones that are your people show them and tell them.

Create, break molds, make noise, stand out and stand up. Be scared, then do it anyway.

Go get your life.

REFERENCES

"Asking for Help." *The Me You Can't See,* season 1, episode 2, Apple TV, 21 May 2021. https://tv.apple.com/us/episode/asking-for-help/umc.cmc.3pztlf7g5zb2d24j3e8vc0prg

Blakeslee, Sandra. "How You See Yourself: Potential for Big Problems" *New York Times,* https://www.nytimes.com/1991/02/07/news/how-you-see-yourself-potential-for-big-problems.html. Accessed 6 July 2021.

"Consequences" *College Drinking.* www.collegedrinkingprevention.gov/Statistics/consequences.aspx. Accessed 3 Jan. 2022.

Dell Technologies. *The Next Era of Human Machine Partnerships.* Institute for the Future, 2017

de Becker, Gavin. *The Gift of Fear.* Bloomsbury Publishing PLC, 2000.

Johnson, Reece. "New Survey Finds Most College Grads Would Change Majors" *Best Colleges,* https://www.bestcolleges.com/blog/college-graduate-majors-survey/. Accessed 22 Aug. 2021.

Joseph, Saumya. "Depression, anxiety rising among U.S. college students" Reuters, https://www.reuters.com/article/

us-health-mental-undergrads-idUKKCN1VJ25Z. Accessed 28 Oct. 2021.

Maroutian, Emily. *The Book of Relief.* Maroutian Entertainment, 2017.

Moss, Rachel. "Inspiring List Reveals Ages Famous People Got Their Big Break, Proves You're Never Too Old For Success" *Huffington Post,* https://www.huffingtonpost.co.uk/ entry/ages-famous-people-got-big-break-facebook-status_ uk_5721f18ee4b0a1e971cb20f6. Accessed 14 Sept. 2021.

Unknown contributors: for the quotes used throughout this book that were not attributed to an author, after extensive research, the author was unknown. Those words are not my own.

ACKNOWLEDGEMENTS

I wrote this book in a global pandemic when I felt lost and lonely. This project got me out of bed in the early mornings to help me reclaim myself. For that, I am grateful to writing and struggling.

Thank you to Kelly Cups for telling me that I can and should write this book. To my Aunt Zibby who holds a Ph.D. in Encouragement and my seester Amanda who always made the time for my questions and calls.

To my friends in Valencia who inspire me in chats over cortados and in the way they fearlessly live their lives. Te quiero un montón.

A big thank you to all of my former students who were the inspiration for this book and who continue to make me proud. To my former MCHS and Summit teaching colleagues: you change lives, certainly mine.

To Jason who wouldn't read my book until I was finished. I get it now.

To all of the college students and faculty who sent me quotes and took the time to be interviewed, I hope I did you proud.

For my forever friends Jessie, Cari, Melissa, Kawen, Delinne, and Rachel. Your friendships were the inspiration for lots of these stories and my foundation as a person.

Pouring one out for "My TN People": Jewell, Davita, Kinsey, and Amanda for being my loyal and unwavering support system 5k miles away.

To Jakey Joe and Luke, being your sister makes me a better person.

Thank you just doesn't seem a big enough phrase for my parents, who raised me with the confidence to express myself and be myself. My life has always felt loud and wildly mine and that's thanks to your love and support that knows no limits.

And to my sweets, who told me over falafel that I was an author. Your belief in me is unwavering as is my love for you. This book is my attempt at making art that will leave young people feeling valued, seen, and loved the way you do for us every day.

The draft of this book was titled "For Sam and Max" so that I could stay encouraged throughout this process. You don't have to go to college to make me proud. You don't even have to get out of bed to make me proud. You are whole and incredible. If you're the only two to read this - it was wildly successful. I love you peanuts.

Printed in the USA
CPSIA information can be obtained
at www.ICGtesting.com
LVHW010415300824
789622LV00007B/333/J